EAT LIKE A LOCAL- LAS VEGAS

Las Vegas Nevada Food Guide

Lindsay N. Klipper

CZYK Publishing Since 2011.

Eat Like a Local

Lock Haven, PA
All rights reserved.
ISBN: 9798607892753

BOOK DESCRIPTION

Are you excited about planning your next trip?

Do you want an edible experience? Would you like some culinary guidance from a local? If you answered yes to any of these questions, then this Eat Like a Local book is for you. Eat Like a Local, Las Vegas by Lindsay N. Klipper offers the inside scoop on some of the best restaurants in Las Vegas, Nevada has to offer. Culinary tourism is an important aspect of any travel experience. Food has the ability to tell you a story of a destination, its landscapes, and culture on a single plate. Most food guides tell you how to eat like a tourist. Although there is nothing wrong with that, as part of the Eat Like a Local series, this book will give you a food guide from someone who has lived at your next culinary destination.

In these pages, you will discover advice on having a unique edible experience. This book will not tell you exact addresses or hours but instead will give you excitement and knowledge of food and drinks from a local that you may not find in other travel food guides.

Eat like a local. Slow down, stay in one place, and get to know the food, people, and culture. By the time you finish this book, you will be eager and prepared to travel to your next culinary destination.

OUR STORY

Traveling has always been a passion of the creator of the Eat Like a Local book series. During Lisa's travels in Malta, instead of tasting what the city offered, she ate at a large fast-food chain. However, she realized that her traveling experience would have been more fulfilling if she had experienced the best of local cuisines. Most would agree that food is one of the most important aspects of a culture. Through her travels, Lisa learned how much locals had to share with tourists, especially about food. Lisa created the Eat Like a Local book series to help connect people with locals which she discovered is a topic that locals are very passionate about sharing. So please join me and: Eat, drink, and explore like a local.

TABLE OF CONTENTS

DEDICATION

This book is dedicated to my mom, who gave me the taste of great food all throughout my childhood in her Italian Kitchen. This book is also dedicated to Trystan, my other half, the foodie in my life who takes cooking at home a little too seriously, but always knows how to make a great presentation.

ABOUT THE AUTHOR

Lindsay is a writing enthusiast, traveler, and foodie. Lindsay was brought up in Long Island, New York under the influence of Italian cooking. Lindsay moved to Sin City during her high school years and stayed to continue her education at the University of Las Vegas, Nevada to become a Special Education Teacher. She has been teaching in this city for about five years. Although her roots stay strong, she considers herself to be a Las Vegas native.

Aside from indulging is casual and fine cuisine, Lindsay loves running, submerging herself in music, and traveling. This past year alone Lindsay has traveled around the world, stopping in 4 different countries, 8 different cities, for 22 days. Her path began in Las Vegas and proceeded route to Italy, Greece, Maldives, and Australia. During her time she immersed herself in the surrounding culture and food deligeses. She experienced everything from chicken souvlaki in Athens to sipping on lemoncello by the Amalfi coast, to traditional pho in Chinatown of Sydney. She was able to not only sightsee historically significant landmarks, but learn about the traditions of each city she had visited. Lindsay enjoys sharing her experiences with her boyfriend who has greatly influenced her passion for traveling and living with a quality of life. As she now takes traveling to the highest priority, she looks forward to continuing her travels around the world.

HOW TO USE THIS BOOK

The goal of this book is to help culinary travelers either dream or experience different edible experiences by providing opinions from a local. The author has made suggestions based on their own knowledge. Please do your own research before traveling to the area in case the suggested locations are unavailable.

Travel Advisories: As a first step in planning any trip abroad, check the Travel Advisories for your intended destination.
https://travel.state.gov/content/travel/en/traveladvisories/traveladvisories.html

FROM THE PUBLISHER

Traveling can be one of the most important parts of a person's life. The anticipation and memories that you have are some of the best. As a publisher of the *Eat Like a Local*, Greater Than a Tourist, as well as the popular *50 Things to Know* book series, we strive to help you learn about new places, spark your imagination, and inspire you. Wherever you are and whatever you do I wish you safe, fun, and inspiring travel.

Lisa Rusczyk Ed. D.
CZYK Publishing

"She serves champagne with
pizza and eats takeout on china"

- Kate Spade

Oh, Las Vegas, Nevada. I know it has its reputation, but this city is just like any other pin on a map. It is someone's home. My home. Don't get me wrong, it does have its perks. You have the best of both worlds. You can get dressed to the nines and go out for a night of luxury at one of the top tier restaurants on the strip, or you can go to your local hole in the wall strip mall that has a line out the door for its spectacular cuisine. Both I have done, both equally has fun. Bonus to all of this, Las Vegas is a 24 hour town. That means all your midnight cravings are cured and your options are endless. Most restaurants around Las Vegas stay open until at least 10pm, therefore you have a lot of leeway when booking your next dinner reservation.

Las Vegas has a very transit and diverse culture. Visitors from across the globe come and want to experience what us locals consider normal. Las Vegas is immersed with the finest dining, top chefs, and the most beautiful restaurant views. With glamour on our side, Las Vegas is deemed one of the most desirable destinations for vacationing and food culture plays a significant role. Tradition, preparation, and presentation is vital for any successful food culture. Las Vegas demonstrates all these attributes while incorporating its own showcasing flare of the town. Dining with an experience is what this town is all about. You are not just having a casual meal, but you are intertwining yourself with the lifestyle of beautiful ambience, food, and entertainment.

Las Vegas
Nevada, USA

Las Vegas Climate

	High	Low
January	59	28
February	66	33
March	72	39
April	81	45
May	90	53
June	102	61
July	107	67
August	104	66
September	96	57
October	83	46
November	70	35
December	60	27

GreaterThanaTourist.com

Temperatures are in Fahrenheit degrees.
Source: NOAA

1. IN FLIGHT FOODIE

Picture this. You are 10,000 ft up in the air, just about that time to relax, read, or fiddle with that app that has been in your phone for a few months now. You start to stretch your legs with a sigh of relief because you know you only have a few more hours until touchdown. As you let a breath out, with champagne in hand, you dream of all the food you are going to divulge on when you land. Maybe you are feeling like greasy food? Five star cuisine? Indian? So many options, yet you only have a few days to explore. Tip number one, do your research. Luckily for you, you are following my advice as you read these words. You will thank me later.

2. GO BIG OR GO HOME

Las Vegas is filled with thousands of options that include different cultures, atmosphere, and taste. You can live the glamorous lifestyle of a celebrity while eating at a michelin star establishment or you can roll up to the local fast food joint on the corner of S. Las Vegas Blvd. Both, tempting options. But the choice is ultimately yours. However, before you drop 150.00 dollars in one night at a restaurant you have never heard of, establish a budget. Schedule out how many "fancy" dinners you want to go to during your stay and how many lunches you wouldn't mind going stingy on.

3. CASINO COMPS

Well, this one isn't entirely food related but it is important. When gambling your paycheck away most casinos will comp your drinks as you play. Comp meaning free. That beautiful, magic, mystical word. Why you ask? They want you to keep playing of course. So the next time you see a waitress roaming the casino floor saying "cocktails" in an unenthused voice, don't be afraid to order a G & T. You must tip obviously, cash or table game chips. Bartenders will even comp your drinks at the hotel bar while you gamble. Typically at each bar their are video poker and black jack games that you can slip in a twenty and play slowly. Regardless of the amount, most bartenders will give drinks for free hoping you will stay a while.

4. DON'T GIVE IN TO TEMPTATION

Whether you never have to watch your weight or you feel like your must workout after every meal you eat, it is definitely beneficial to not give in to every food establishment you see! Vegas can be overwhelming. As you walk through the glitz and glamour there are ice cream stands, burger joints, and coffee shops everywhere you turn. The worst part is, they all look appealing because they each have their own flare to pull you in. I got to give it to my mom for this one "you don't want to spoil your dinner." Don't show up to your 8pm reservation on a full stomach about to spend $30.00 a head.

5. THE BARTENDER IS YOUR FRIEND

If you are planning to run a tab for the night, it may be in your best interest to tip the bartender before your drinks. Faster service and stronger drinks always makes for a good night out. If you can avoid waiting in a crowd three people deep before getting your next G & T, you might as well work the tips to your advantage.

6. I'VE GOT A COUPON

One of the easiest ways to save money on a meal is to use coupons. Many hotels provide coupons with your stay. Why? To keep you in the hotel. Typically coupon books are handed to you when checking in, however they can also be located in your room. Save on the meal, spend more at the tables! Aside from food, these coupon books also offer discounts for entertainment, drinks, and gmabling. Looking up discount on the web is another great way to find coupons and you would be surprised to find what the top restaurants and hotels have to offer.

7. PLAYERS CARD

No, you don't have to play to get a Players Card. No, it does not cost you anything. Players Cards are typically used to record time for when you play slots or table games to rack up points for dining and shows. However, if you have a Players Card at the hotel you are feasting at chances are that restaurant provides a small discount. Especially with buffets. To get a Players Card, just go to your hotel's information desk to retrieve and save!

Side note, most of the hotels are run by the same corporation and are sister properties to one another. Therefore, if you get a players card at one hotel and then decide to dine at another your players card could still get your discounts.

8. DON'T BE OVERWHELMED

Menus can be overwhelming. You think you just have your starters, your entrees, and your desserts. But, there is so much more. Most upscale restaurants split their menus into meats, seafood, and pastas. The list goes on. Sometimes it feels like you are holding a library book instead of a menu. My advice, look up the menu beforehand to get a feel for what you are craving. That way you aren't the only one at the table feeling rushed, flipping through page after page deciding on what you should commit to.

9. STAY HYDRATED

Before you indulge in everything Las Vegas has to offer, remember rule one. Always stay hydrated. This city is a desert, and it's dry. Water is always free, so make sure you drink a lot of it before journeying to your seven o'clock reservation five hotels down the road. Not to mention it is always beneficial to stay hydration if alcohol is in the equation. The only water you won't find free is the fancy bottles that are lying around your hotel room.

10. FIND THE RIGHT TIME

Heads up, Vegas will always be crowded no matter the time. But, you can avoid "rush hours" by dining at a time that is not as slammed. If you are an early riser, more power to you as you will have no problem finding a breakfast spot. Breakfast rush hours range from 9-11am, so if you are looking to get a head start to the day plan on eating prior to then. Lunch varies and can be anywhere from 12-3pm. Lunch is always dependent on what activities tourists plan for the day, so you have more leeway to not catch the crowd. However, popular dinner times can range from 8-10pm as everyone wants to get a meal in before clubs open. Therefore, if you aren't into the party scene it would be wise to plan for an early dinner.

11. PULL OUT THE RED CARPET

If you are looking to plan out one meal of the day, dinner is a must. Dinner is more than just a time to consume calories, it is an experience. Some people spend hours of planning around a two-three hour of sitting at a dimly lit establishment paying top dollar for tapas. However, the scheduling is totally worth it. Research your restaurant, understand the atmosphere, and dress appropriately. You don't want to over dress, but be careful of under dressing too. Most restaurants mention their dress code on their website, it's worth it to take a peek. Just don't get too serious with it, after all this is Vegas. Rhinestones and sequins are always welcome.

12. RESERVATION FOR TWO

The worst feeling in the world is when you walk up to the hostess on an empty stomach, dressed to the nines, just to find out that the restaurant was fully booked and you have to wait over two hours for a table. You panic but you don't want to wait. So, you end up at the nearest restaurant that has an empty table. Distatified and disappointed you couldn't experience that shrimp tartare you have been thinking about since noon. Solution? I know Vegas is all about gambling, but play it safe. Make a reservation. Not to mention making a reservation is easier than ever. Most reservations can be booked online through the restaurant's website. Some reservation websites that are linked to hotels also offer discounts for making a reservation online.

13. FIND YOUR VIBE

There are dozens of hotels on the strip. Each with their own unique style and theme. If you are looking to dine for a family night of fun, New York New York is the way to go. Explore the streets of the Big Apple without the hussel and bussel. After splitting a pizza pie at the New York Pizzeria, take a ride on the indoor / outdoor roller coaster.

Meanwhile, if you are looking for more of a romantic night out, look no further than the Bellagio. After enjoying a stroll through Bellagio's themed conservatory, you can have romantic Italian cuisine dine in experience at Lago while watching the breath taking view of the Bellagio fountain show.

On the other hand, if you are out with a group of friends looking for a casual hangout spot, look no further than Beerhaus at The Park. This is the perfect eatery for grabbing a few and playing bar games. Beerhaus also has a fairy lit outdoor patio to set that "come stay a while" vibe.

14. NAME DROPPERS

Now, if you love name-dropping for boasting points. Vegas is your playground. There are so many world renowned chefs that make Las Vegas their home to their beautifully crafted food and ambience that create the perfect breakfast, lunch, or dinner experience. Just to name a few, WolfGang Puck,

Gordan Ramsey, and Joel Robuchon have stunning restaurants throughout the strip. So choose wisely.

15. WOLFGANG PUCK

Alright, well since you asked, let's name drop a few. WolfGang Puck has restaurants located all over the map. If you are looking for a more intimate dining experience, I recommend Spago by WolfGang Puck at the Bellagio. Spago patio is feet away from the iconic Bellagio fountain and presents the perfect view for an evening night out you and your date will not forget. But, let's be real. Not all of us can afford Spago prices. In any case, my personal local favorite is Players Locker By WolfGang Puck in Downtown Summerlin. Fun atmosphere, with amazing chefs, equals a great evening out. Not to mention, they have a killer drink and food happy hour menu. Want a real recommendation? Try their house margarita. I promise it will compliment any dish you order.

16. GORDAN RAMSEY

Like all the rest, Gordan Ramsey gives you options and offers a taste to all wallet types. If you want to be apart of the highlife, visit Gordon Ramsay Steak at the Paris. You will be transported from the French culture to the British cuisine. Try classic cultural dish Beef Wellington that is the spotlight of the menu as well as other water watering meats all presented on rolling trolleys. However, if meat is not your thing, Gordon Ramsey Fish and Chips located at the Linq is a to go counter that packs a flavorful punch. The menu is simple, but the bite is beautiful.

17. JOEL ROBUCHON

Okay, last name dropping recommendation. Joel Robuchon at the MGM Grand feels like home. And when I say home, I mean a mansion. Entering this elaborately designed restaurant is if you have walked into the home of a wealthy businessman that has asked you to stay for dinner. With sparkling chandeliers, purple curtains, and monochrome tiles, you will feel like royalty dining in French style. And if you think the food is not as intricate at its interior design, you would be heavily mistaken. Joel

Robuchon highlight the Le Sphere, which is a sugar sphere filled with blackberry sorbet with the enhancing flavors of lemons and violet cream.

18. LEAVIN' THE STRIP

If you truly want to live the local life and the neighborhood, look beyond S. Las Vegas Blvd. There is so much more than just your local chain restaurants. Different sectors of Las Vegas provide you with their own cultures and dining experiences. The most popular places to go are Fremont Street, Downtown Summerlin, Town Square, and Chinatown. Each provides a completely different type of nightlife and eastery options. The choice is yours to find which sector best fits your nightlife!

19. NIGHT OUT WITHOUT BREAKING THE BANK

It is a general Vegas local rule that if you are looking to have a fun night out without spending your paycheck, Fremont Street is generally cheaper. Fremont Street has a prethala of casual dining choices that satisfy any craving. The inexpensive cost just

means you will have more money to spend on drinks.
Bonus, the drinks are less expensive too!

20. FERMONT FINDS

Let me expand. Interested in people watching? It's
hard to describe the culture of Fremont Street as it is
like nonother. If you are looking for an adventurous
night out you may begin your night at Oscar's
Steakhouse at the Plaza. As you enjoy your mayor's
signature martini while waiting for your delectable
aged steak, you find yourself looking out the iconic
glass dome that gives you a perfect view of the
Fermont lights. After dinner you may find yourself
ordering cocktails from one of the many outside bars
while making your way to watch one live music. Or
even more adventurous, zip line down the street
itself! As the night digresses and you are craving a
midnight snack, you may end your night at the nearest
Nacho Daddy, where a side of queso is a must!

21. DON'T FORGET DOWNTOWN SUMMERLIN

Downtown Summerlin, located just twenty five minutes from the strip, is an outside upscale mall with numerous food options from five star restaurants to casual eateries. Enjoy retail therapy or a movie between courses while you are there too! A couple of my top picks to eat are WolfGang Puck Players Locker, Trattoria Reggiano, and Magginos. Now, I have already name dropped WolfGang Puck Players Locker, so let's skip to Trattoria Reggiano. On the corner of Park Centre Drive, in the heart of the outside mall, there is a quaint Italian gem that serves the most delicious pasta specialties from Spaghetti al Filetto di Pomodoro to Penne a la Vodka. Just in case that menu is not to your liking, Magginos at Downtown Summerlin always has a way of making your party feel like one of a kind. If you are celebrating anything in particular, the servers at Magginos will pamper you and your guests.

With kids? There is also Dave and Busters that caters to all parts of the family. With a massive arcade area filled with a variety of classic and modern games, you kids will be set to spend at least a couple of hours on the digital screens. Meanwhile, the other half of the establishment emphasizes the adults including a sports bar and restaurant. The sports bar side offers a classic American menu, beers on draft, and a television everywhere you turn. All the standard necessities for watching the big game!

22. TRADITIONAL IN CHINA TOWN

Experience the three mile stretch around Spring Mountain Road for the most local Asian cuisine. There are approximately 150 restaurants and 6 grocery stores within this small radius. There are also two strip malls that house a majority of these food establishments. Let's just say you won't gp starved in this neck of the woods!

If you are looking for an interactive dining experience, Chubby Cattle, in Chinatown has a build your own Chinese hotpot that is delivered to your table via conveyor belt. In the center of this "Chinese fondue" is a delicious broth with your choosing of uncooked sides, thinly sliced meats, and seafood. Pick what you will and chefs will cook it to perfection!

23. DID SOMEONE SAY "BUY ONE GET ONE?"

Oh my food coma! Welcome to the city of buffet. Each hotel has their own buffet incorporating their own unique twist. Buffets are perfect because they have a little something for everyone. If you are looking for a casual buffet that does just that, try out the Carnival World Buffet at the Rio. This buffet is known for his diverse food selection ranging from Asian, to Seafood, to Mexican. If you are looking for more of an upscale style, Wicked Spoon at the Cosmopolitan will not disappoint. The platter presentation at this buffet will give you the feel of a michelin star restaurant. The best part about these buffets are the discounts. Another top notch buffet is located at the Aria. This buffet offers a revolving selection of fresh seafood, classic American cuisine, and delectable desserts. The best perk to this buffet is it offers an all you can drink special for an up charge of twenty dollars. This includes mimosas, bloody mary's, premium beer and wine, and classic margaritas. With a deal like this it may be wise to ride share home.

24. THE HAPPIEST OF HOURS

There are countless amounts of Happy Hours offered all throughout the Vegas strip. I am not just talking about the small corner bars you may see making your way to your dinner reservation. Every hotel, five to one star, has their own happy hours. Typically 4-6pm, if you are lucky until 7pm. Nothing a little google research can't find. Search your hotel stay restaurants and you will be happily surprised at what each establishment has to offer!

First off to mention, Allegro at the Wynn has happy hour Saturday's and Sunday's from 3-5:30pm. In addition to discounts at their pizza bar, Allegro offers all you can drink draft beers for twenty-five dollars. Estiatorio Milos at the Cosmopolitan has more of an accessible happy hour, daily from 5 to 7pm and keeps its specials around the twelve dollar mark.

25. DRINK LIKE A LOCAL

Less than ten minutes from S. Las Vegas Blvd. lies a speakeasy like cocktail lounge and restaurant called Herbs and Rye. This proobilitionary vibed lounge has the perfect hisotrically classic cocktails that is every bit worth the price. Added bonus, they have happy hour on speciality drink specials from Monday through Saturday. I suggest making a reservation before arriving as this place gets pretty packed.

Frankie's Tiki Room is another Las Vegas local classic featuring an incredible drink menu and an under the sea interior design.The specailtiy cocktails incorpoarte exoictic rum drinks including a drink that will be presented on fire. This bar is great to mingle and lounge with friends for an evening out. The vibe is always lively and busy. Side note, make sure to make a reservation. It may be tough getting a table to seat your party without one.

26. PARTY LIKE IT'S 1922

Girls in glitzzy get ups, the sound of soft R&B playing, and gold embellished decor. Take a time warp into the 1920's when low waisted dresses and bobbed hairstyles were in fashion. If you are looking to feel like you have entered the era of Great Gatsby, try out the sophisticated Rosina Cocktail Lounge in The Palazzo. Rosina has a speciality menu that features Shak en, Stirred, and Bubbly drinks that bartenders are experts in concocting. With classic hand crafted cocktails, a champagne call button at your service, and a secret menu provided only when brought up to your server, you will feel like you have entered an exclusive social club for the elite.

27. IT'S GAME TIME

Looking for a bar to kick back and watch a few games while being surrounded by a bucket of beers and wings? Twins Peaks, located in the heart of the strip, is a two level lodge like sports bar that is so substantial it houses a 39 ft climbing wall. And, yes,you can actually climb it. Enjoy the American dream of burgers and bar food while kicking back and mingling with the friendly bartenders, while putting your paycheck on your favorite team.

28. NOT LIKE ANY OTHER FOOD COURT

Sometimes you are just in the mood for that food court feel. You know what I am talking about, the gallery walk you do at a food court when you don't know what you are in the mood for. Fingers crossed for free samples. The food court at Fashion Show Mall on the strip is one of my favorites. Why? Well, because it is on the third floor of the mall so you get a killer view of the strip. This food court has indoor and outdoor seating and is perfect when you need an intermission from retail therapy. Not to mention, its food selection is more than just your classics. The food court features India Marsala, The Habit Burger Grill, and Opa! Of Greece.

29. HANGOVER HOTSPOTS

Although nothing beats going to Denny's about after a night out just to people watch, Las Vegas has many hotspots to fulfill your hangover needs. Are you running late to the airport after a night of too much fun and need something on the go? Eggslut at the Cosmopolitan is your sarver. With countless egg options your desire for something greasy, yet delicious will be satisfied. However, if you are enjoying your hangover fest with a group of friends, Hash House A Go Go at the Linq will provide you with an all American classic breakfast with a wide Mimosa selection that will hit the spot. Keep in mind these portions are huge, so you may want to consider sharing.

30. LOCAL BREAKFAST CLASSICS

As you wake up in your crisp white sheets amongst the silence of the strip, there are a few things you need to know. Breakfast can be a crowded time, as everyone is waking up late from the same excuse the night before. But you were smarter than all of them, you downed a liter of water before bed. You are feeling like sunshine, and you don't want to be amongst the hungover zombies. Well, in this case, try out these local Vegas classics. Omelette House, Ichabod's, and the Peppermill Restaurant and Lounge are all local hotspots that will satisfy any breakfast burrito craving.

Omelette House pulls off that old Vegas vibe featuring old-time pictures surrounding the interior. With big portions, every omelette option in existence, and unlimited drip coffee, it is safe to say you will be stuffed until lunch. Ichabod's is as local as it can get. It is located less than fifteen minutes from the strip and features an old vintage style including a piano bar and live music at night. The breakfast is at the right price and all American with friendly serves that make you feel right at home. The Peppermill Restaurant and Lounge is a most stop breakfast spot with a laid back atmosphere. The weight time at this restaurant does get pretty heavy, so plan accordingly!

31. MORE MIMOSA PLEASE

Bottomless mimosas are the game? Andiron Steak & Sea is the name. Located in Downtown Summerlin, this upscale brunch spot is perfect for wearing your Sunday best. With bottomless bubbles, a Bloody Mary bar, and the perfect avocado toast, I don't think you could possibly ask for anything more. High vaulted ceiling, bright open windows, and a white atmosphere makes for a perfect start to a beautiful Sunday.

32. FOR THE CAFFEINE ADDICT

Do you like Harry Potter? Do you like Coffee? Do you like those two concepts together? If you said yes to all these questions then Bad Owl Coffee is for you. Aside from being Harry Potter themed, this coffee shop has such a unique menu of coffee and pastries. My personal favorite is the Roasted Almond Latte. Did I mention there are real sliced almonds at the bottom? There specialty coffees compliment their delectable pastries. Side note, you can get a perfect flat lay instagram shot with your coffee as each wooden table is engraved with a quote from Harry Potter. There are two locations in Las Vegas, so the choice is yours!

33. MIDNIGHT SNACKIN'

In search of the perfect midnight snack? You have already had dinner, drinks, and gambled, yet you have been working up an appetite for a little something something. There are your classic options of McDonalds and Denny's. However, if you are looking for an option that is a little unconventional White Castle is also located stone throws away from the Venetian. White Castle, incase there are those of you who do not know, is credited to be America's first fast food chain and is home to the Original

Slider. This slide may be bite sized, but that just means you can justify ordering multiples!

34. INSTAGRAM WORTHY

Want some down time away from the strip? But, also need a pick me up? When you arrive at Gabi's Coffee & Bakery on Spring Mountain Road, you are entering a bookworm's paradise. It is decorated with the most welcoming natural features incorporating a greenhouse in the middle of the establishment. Sit on the three tier wooden benches and put your legs up as you admire the greenery, edison bulbs, and of course your delectable meal. Gabi's has a variety of coffee lover classics as well as seasonal handmade pastries and baked goods.

35. FIND YOUR INNER ITALIAN

Antipasto, pasta, pizza, the works. I got you covered. So, let's start off small. If you are looking for the most authentic Italian deli in town, hands down you need to go to Cugino's. It is in this small strip center across the street from University of

Nevada, Las Vegas on S. Maryland Parkway. I promise you will have no regrets. As I said, I am an Italian New Yorker so I know what real pizza is supposed to taste like. However, if you and your party are looking for more family style authentic taste with a dine in experience, Italian American Club is my go to. Aside from traditional dishes, Italian American Club offers an Old Vegas feel as well as live music. Now if you are more modern style with a view, Panevino on Via Antonio Ave. is your place. With open floor to ceiling windows pointing at the strip, you and your sweetheart with definitely want to stay long enough for dessert.

36. SPICE OF INDIA

Easiest category yet. You want authentic? Oh, I will give you authentic. Mt. Everest India's Cuisine is family owned presenting a variety of dishes from North India. From dishes like Chicken Tikki Masala to Butter Chicken Curry, there is no need to travel any further than Las Vegas' backyard for authentic Indian food. Keep in mind when planning your meals around this hotspot, they are only open for a lunch buffet and dinner.

37. GO TO THE GREEK

Yassou, a little less than twenty minutes from the strip, is a traditional deli style Greek cafe. This family run business is the perfect spot if you are looking to enjoy lunch where the locals do. There menu is filled with gyro platters, pita sandwiches and salads, so you know you can't go wrong. And if you have a little room left over, try the rice pudding or baklava for a sweet treat!

38. I'LL HAVE A SIDE OF GUACAMOLE

In the heart of Downtown Summerlin there is a Mexican restaurant that represents traditional and modern flare. Inside is beautifully decorated with bright colored tiles, greenery, and an indoor fountain. This restaurant has two levels, so I recommend eating upstairs for a pretty view. While dining here, it feels more like a fiesta than anything. mariachi musicians and waitresses in traditional attire create a welcoming and festive atmosphere for any occasion. Bonus, happy hour on weekends are extended! Saturdays are from 11 a.m. to 7 p.m. and Sundays are from 10 a.m. to 7 p.m. I guess it's five o'clock somewhere?

39. FOR THE SEA FOODIE

You have a few options. Just kidding, you have tons of options. It all depends on what side of town you want to experience your king crab. If you are looking to dine in the suburbs, Andiron Steak & Sea has oysters, maine lobsters, and shrimp to cure your fresh seafood craving. WIth elegant atmosphere and sophisticated culture this is the perfect place for a romantic night out. If you wish to stay on the strip, Lakeside at the Wynn prepares exquisite dishes like mahi mahi, lobster risotto, and leeks featured on their Hwaiann curated menu. Along with the exquisite taste of the served oven-roasted lobster, this award winning restaurant is located right on the Lake of Dreams making it an exceptional spot for dining.

40. STOPPIN' FOR SUSHI

Now if you are looking to spend a pretty penny on sushi, Mizumi at the Wynn is definitely a crowd pleaser. Mizumi offers sushi and sashimi, not to mention the restaurant has a teppanyaki room. This restaurant sits open to Wynn's beautiful garden incorporating a soothing waterfall for a romantic experience. However if you are looking for more of a casual AYCE vibe, Yama Sushi is your restaurant. Don't let the location of a strip mall deceive you, this restaurant has one of the best rolls in town. I will warn you, it does get packed so make sure to plan for an hour wait if you are with a big party.

41. I SEE LONDON, I SEE FRANCE

Did you know that the Eiffel Tower in Las Vegas is half scale to the one in Paris, France? The Eiffel Tower in Las Vegas is about 540 feet high. If you are interested in having a French experience without paying the expense of paying Europe prices, have a date night out at the Paris Las Vegas Hotel. Begin your French excursion at none other than the Eiffel Tower Restaurant itself. This elegant restaurant on the eleventh floor of the Eiffel Tower overlooks the impeccable view of the Bellagio fountain and Las Vegas strip. Combining this view with outstanding service and traditional French cuisine will make for a night out you will not forget. Some of the restaurant's signature dishes include Beef Wellington, Roasted

Rack of Lamb, and Grand Seafood Platters. Each dish will provide you will the taste of France without the hassle of an international flight.

42. FOR THE STEAK LOVER

You have two choices. Well you have more than two choices, but I am only going to mention two. I have been to multiple steakhouses around town and by far Del Frisco's wins hand down. Not only do they have an impeccable wine selection, but the process in which they cook their steaks are top notch. However, I realize not everyone wants to venture off the strip, so my second recommendation is STK Steakhouse at the Cosmopolitan. If you are looking for a modern take on a premium quality steakhouse, STK Steakhouse is where you need to make your next reservation. The atmosphere in this restaurant is like nonother, it provides guests with a lounge feel with a premium food experience. STK also adversities an excellent Happy Hour with half off drinks and discounted bites.

43. THE IN'S AND OUT'S

Going to In-N-Out is a necessity for someone traveling to Las Vegas. You think it would be your standard fast food joint, but it is so much more. I have seen a line of of fifteen cars wait in the In-N-Out Burger line. The menu is very simplistic including a few options of burgers and fries, however look up items on their "secret menu" for different styles, sauces, and shakes.

44. FEELIN' LIKE FRIED FOOD

Another fast food staple is Canes. Canes has another simplistic menu, but they are experts at what they do offer. Fried chicken strips, texas toast, and fries. Not to mention, they have a special canes sauce that compliments everything to a tee. It is perfect for a stop and go experience between your bigger courses.

45. SHHH! IT'S A SECRET

Hidden on the third floor of the Cosmopolitan there lies a secret. A secret pizzeria that is. To the average eye, this casual eatery does not exist. But to the curious eye who follows the hidden record lined hallway, will find a New York pizza lovers sanctuary. The best part? They offer pizza by the slice! Not to mention, they provide a wine and eber list to compliment your personalized pie.

46. WHEN ONE DOOR OPENS

Greene St. Kitchen at the Palms has the most unique and eye catching entrance I have ever experienced. In fact, the first time I came across Green St. Kitchen I didn't even realize it was a restaurant. The front of the restaurant is disguised as a small arcade. Pacman, Donkey Kong,Ping-Pong, you know the works. On the center of one of the back walls is a red Coca-Cola freezer door that is really the entrance to a street style paradise featuring signature cocktails, seafood, and American cuisine. You are completely transformed into a new dimension as you walk through this New York Soho style establishment. Their menu offers an innovative twist on Seafood and American cuisine while incorporating the most tasteful foods.

47. DINNER WITH A VIEW

Have you ever wondered what it would be like to see the strip from a 360 degree view all while enjoying a quality meal? Well, if you answered yes. I have answered your prayers. Top of the World at the Stratosphere is located on the 106th floor of the hotel. This restaurant rotates 360 degrees every 80 minutes, therefore providing you with the most sunsational view of the Las Vegas Strip. The menu consists of fresh seafood and premium meats as well as a delicious dessert menu. My personal favorite is the Warm Butter Cake with compliments a variety of berries and vanilla bean ice cream.

48. LOTUS SIAM

In the most unlikely location lies a true Las Vegas treasure. Lotus of Siam, which houses the James-Beard Foundation award-winning chef Saipin Chutima, is the best Thai restaurant in town. I kid you not, this place is so popular, I needed to make dinner reservations a month out because they were completely booked. Luckily, they have an in house bar that makes a wait feel like nothing. This menu has something for everyone. From garlic prawns to fried wontons to creamy yellow curry, you will want to family style and taste everything presented on the table.

49. THE STUDY OF GELATO

Gelatology is a measly twenty minutes from the strip and carries big flavor. This gelato shop is worth the travel as the flavor's creamy consistency takes your taste buds on a trance. After one visit, you will be wanting to come back multiple times within your stay. Everyday Gelatology's menu changes with unique flavors from Ube to Sweet Cream to the classics. Best part, they always post their flavors on their instagram, so you know what to look forward to! Side note, their cappuccinos are just as good as their creamy frozen delights!

50. HYPED ON SUGAR

Candy drinks, colored hamburger buns, and goblets of drinks. If you have a sweet tooth, this is the place for you. Sugar Factory at Fashion Show showcases a Chocolate Lounge on the upper level and a full service restaurant experience on the lower. Of course this fun and bright designed restaurant has a full service menu featuring all things American. The drinks at Sugar Factory are just as unique as their interior decor. Did I mention lollipops and gummy worms are incorporated in your drinks? Goblets of alcohol are typically shared amongst at least two and make for a great photo opt moment.

BONUS TIPS: JACKPOT!

BONUS TIP 1: I FEEL LIKE I FORGOT SOMETHING

I know packing tips can be really obvious. Bring a toothbrush, toothpaste. Well, duh. What you do need to know is you must bring sunscreen. Las Vegas is hot and typically always sunny. You don't want your trip ruined from chance of hanging poolside without coverage and end up looking like a lobster the rest of your trip.

Speaking of coverage, bring a cover up for the pool. I know this may sound common, but you don't want to be the one person walking through the casino floor, heading back to your room on the twenty-second floor, with just your bathing suit because you only packed your black bikini and flip flops.

BONUS TIP 2: TEMPTING, BUT DON'T DO IT

You walked three miles of crowds and casinos, exhausted and wanting to be in your cushy hotel room king sized bed. On the journey up all you are thinking about is how cozy you are going to be when you take off your sneakers that have been giving you blisters on the back of your feet. As you finally lay down on your precious cloud of a mattress, you realize your stomach is growling.

Well, now what? You roam through the hotel room to munch on something and all you can find are items from the snack bar. Tempting? But, don't do it. You can be charged 6 dollars for a water that is 89 cents down the street at Walgreens. Take my advice. First stop of the trip, go to Walgreens or CVS. There are a few locations spread out throughout the strip. Save yourself some unnecessary money spent.

BONUS TIP 3: EXPLORE DURING THE DAY

Las Vegas strip is bigger than you think. So if you assume that you can explore the whole boulevard in one night, you are sadly mistaken. In that case, get your steps in during the day and wander at night. This way you are more comfortable with your bearings even after a couple of signature cocktails. Additional tip, bring a pair of comfortable shoes to journey in during the day. I know, I know, it's not the most fashionable option. However, save your "beauty is pain" motto for the evening when you have to wear your skin tight dresses or uncomfortable suites.

There are also so many other options to explore than hanging around the strip all day. One, visit Las Vegas sign. Technically it is not located in the heart of the strip, so you will have to travel roughly five minutes away. If you are looking to get further out, Red Rock Canyon about thirty minutes away offers gorgeous hikes and trails that you can spend all day wandering. Hiking too boring for you? There is also an incredible zip lining experience in Boulder City that will provide you will epic view and a memorable experience.

BONUS TIP 4: STAY FOR LUNCH, LEAVE FOR DINNER

If you are interested in going to top notch restaurants without paying top dollar, check out the lunch menu. Odds are it is substantially more reasonably priced and the food is coming from the same kitchen. Estiatorio Milos at the Cosmopolitan is a prime example. You can get a three course lunch meal for about $25. Meanwhile, during dinner these you could be paying that for just one dish.

BONUS TIP 5: LET'S JUST SHARE SOMETHING

Vegas style is definitely over the top and food is no exception. Sometimes the presentation and dishes are way too much for one. Consider sharing before between meals. Not to mention, nothing is more of a nuisance than lugging around leftovers all day because you do not want to venture back to your room to drop half a sandwich off in the fridge. Save your calories and your wallet!

BONUS TIP 6: I JUST WANT A BITE

If you are someone that loves to "taste" everything on the menu, tapas are perfect for you. Tapas are small appetizers that originated in Spain, but the concept has travelled to Las Vegas full force. Jaleo at the Cosmopolitan is just one of many tapa options.

Prepare for a Spanish feast when walking into Jaleo.
Although Tapas are offered, Jaleo offers a wide
variety of Spanish cuisine that includes your classic
fajitas, enchiladas, and queso. Paella, one of Jaleo's
signature dishes is cooked-over a wood-burning grill
giving the flavor true authenticity.

BONUS TIP 7: RIDESHARE > TAXIS

There is so much transportation around the Las
Vegas strip and everyone is trying to get in and out at
all times. Lyfts, Ubers, and Taxis all provide the same
service, but which is better? More efficient? And
cheaper, of course? Well, this is a tough one because
each has its pros and cons. Typically, Lyfts and Ubers
are more convenient and less expensive. Each hotel
has a rideshare pick up outside their establishment
that makes it easy for arrivals and departures.
However, these areas can also get very chaotic during
peak hours as everyone is leaving from the same area.
In this case, taxis and cabs seems to have more
convenience over ride sharing and may be worth the
extra couple of bucks. Rideshares also have peak
hours on the strip. This means that the expensive for

your transportation from point A to point B will cost you an extra dime. Keep this in mind the next time you are only three blocks away from your destination and about to hit that pay button on your phone.

BONUS TIP 8:   WELCOME TO THE SUPPERCLUB

Mayfair is new to the block. Block meaning the Las Vegas Strip. It provides so much more than your typical dining experience. Located at the Bellagio, this supperclub also promotes an "after dark" experience with live musical talents and performances. Mayfair at the Bellagio Hotel and Casino offers a pre theater dinner menu and dinner menu. Both with superb selections that will compliment the entertainment of your night.

BONUS TIP 9:   HOW SHOULD WE SPLIT THIS?

You are out with your entourage, done up and ready for a big night out. Your plan is to splunge and have a semi fine dining experience before slowly losing your sophistication in alcohol for the rest of the night. At the table, appetizers are being ordered, drinks are being poured, and you decide you have room for dessert. The bill comes and the waitress does not know who to pass it to. Oh. no. Here comes the awkward conversation of "Do you have cash?" "How can we split this?" Suggestion, if you are planning a Las Vegas weekend with friends decide on a common digital wallet app that you all agree upon. That way when that bill comes everyone is prepared to send one person their fair share.

BONUS TIP 10: MAP OUT YOUR ROUTE

Las Vegas Blovendard is much bigger than you actually think. Why? Well, because it is not a straight shot. You have to dodge solicitors, stumbling pedestrians, and casino entrance ways while walking. Make sure your route of the night makes sense. You don't want to make a dinner reservation at the Stratosphere knowing you will be going to a concert at the Mandalay Bay a couple hours later. Those two hotels are on the polar ends of the strip, or might as well be the opposite ends of the Earth. Walking part of the Strip is fun, but you do not want the travel to your next destination to be the full duration of your evening out.

Speaking of mapping out your route, keep in mind you are surrounded by very tall sky scrape like buildings. Therefore, chances are your cell phone service will not be superb. Another reason to know your route. You don't want to be walking aimlessly around the strip just to realize you have been walking in the wrong direction for twenty minutes.

BONUS TIP 11:   KNOW YOUR DRINKS

Before you order that Raspberry Sunset with a twist for 20 dollars a pop. Know exactly what you are going to order, before you make the splunge. Don't be afraid to ask the bartender about your drink or even ask for a sample. Bartenders will be happy to serve you, as long as you tip of course. Stick with the types of liquor that you know and are familiar with. Most likely these will be the drinks you will be most satisfied with when you get the tab at the end of the night.

BONUS TIP 12: DINNER AND A SHOW

Now that I have got you covered for your breakfast, lunch, and dinner. Not to mention, your happy hour and dessert scheduling. You have to decide what activity you wish to partake in after your feasting is over. Most tourists love shows. Just like our dining selection, there is so much variety to show night life. Vegas has stand up comedians, concerts, and Cirque du Soleil shows occurring daily for your entertainment. However, just like anything else they are expensive. Major tip for saving money, use Tix4Tonight when purchasing your entertainment of choice. Tickets4Tonight has discounts on shows, attractions, and even top restaurants. What is the catch? Well, you have to buy the voucher for night of, meaning you have to be more of the spontaneous time to really take advantage of what Tickets4Tonight has to offer. The have about nin stores around the Vegas Valley to pick up your tickets and the best part is you can check out their deals online prior to taking a trip out to see what they have to offer.

OTHER RESOURCES:

www.groupon.com- For Restaurant / Event Discounts

www.tripadvisor.com- For Customer Reviews

www.opentable.com- For Reservations

https://www.tix4tonight.com/- For Half Priced
    Entertainment

READ OTHER BOOKS BY CZYK PUBLISHING

Greater Than a Tourist- St. Croix US Birgin Islands USA: 50 Travel Tips from a Local by Tracy Birdsall

Greater Than a Tourist- Toulouse France: 50 Travel Tips from a Local by Alix Barnaud

Children's Book: *Charlie the Cavalier Travels the World* by Lisa Rusczyk

Eat Like a Local

Follow *Eat Like a Local on* Amazon.
Join our mailing list for new books
http://bit.ly/EatLikeaLocalbooks

Made in United States
Cleveland, OH
21 February 2026

33677515R00049